THE TURRA COO

Robert Paterson.

THE TURRA COO

*A Legal Episode in the Popular Culture of
North-East Scotland*

Alexander Fenton

ABERDEEN UNIVERSITY PRESS
Member of Maxwell Macmillan Pergamon Publishing Corporation

First published 1989
Aberdeen University Press
© Alexander Fenton 1989

British Library Cataloguing in Publication Data
Fenton, Alexander
    The Turra Coo: a legal episode in the popular culture of
    North-East Scotland.
    1. Scotland. Grampian Region. Turriff, 1910–1936
    I. Title
    941.2'25

    ISBN 0 08 037729 7

Printed in Great Britain
The University Press
Aberdeen

Contents

List of Illustrations

Foreword

The town of Turriff lies in the heart of fine farming country in Buchan, which used to be part of Aberdeenshire but is now part of Grampian Region. The first thing to catch the eye is the number of attractive red-sandstone buildings, different from the slate and granite of its North-East neighbours. Its Cross, in the same stone, greets visitors entering from Queen's Road. Put up in 1865, it replaces an original 20 foot cross erected in 1557 soon after Turriff became a Burgh of Barony.[1] It is known far and wide through a rhyme I learned as a boy in the neighbouring parish of Auchterless, marking the fact that the town is the same distance from Aberdeen as from Elgin:

> Choose ye, chise ye,
> At the Cross o' Turra,
> Fidder tae gang tae Aiberdeen
> Or Elgin o' Mora'.

Turriff has also gained fame in other proverbs and sayings. When Helen Beaton wrote *At the Back o' Benachie* in 1915, she included the phrase: 'Far are ye gaun: Turra! Far sorra idder.' Since then, 'Turra! Far sorra idder' has become an almost automatic answer if someone asks where you are going. The *Scottish National Dictionary* has a special entry under *Turra*, recording three items. One is the phrase 'to ride to Turra', meaning to be merry or elated. It goes back to 1804, when William Tarras commented in his *Poems* that the people of Turriff were famous for merriment: 'hence he is said to be riding to Turra, who is merry.' The phrase is no longer remembered. Another entry, quoting the *Aberdeen Press & Journal* for 16 December 1960, gives a nickname for the people of Turriff: a 'Turra tattie' or a 'Turra neep'. A third logs an outline of the Turra Coo story, about which this present book is concerned. And Turriff is known far and wide also through the song, The Barnyards o' Delgaty, which begins with the lines:

> As I gaed doon be Turra Market,
> Turra Market for tae fee . . .

Sayings and songs are sound mechanisms for keeping places in mind. So also are historical events, which sometimes gain an almost independent life of their own. For most of the time, Turriff has been a place of peace, though according to a Report of the Inspector of Prisons in 1837,[2] its shoemakers were notorious for being ready to fight. It is true that in the 1790s, souters were the most numerous of the tradesmen in the town. There were 36 of them, closely followed by the weavers who numbered 34. Their fighting qualities may have been enhanced by visits to the 15 sellers of ale and whisky that served a town population of 701 at that period, though the drouths of the surrounding countryside would have made good use of them as well.[3] But there have been periods of disturbance too, that brought fame to Turriff, involving the town in the politics of the nation.

The first was in 1639, when the town was a centre of Covenanting activities. It was occupied by the Earl of Montrose with 800 troops in February, for a time. Three months later Royalist forces overcame the Turriff Covenanters, making themselves 'maisters of the villadge'. This event came to be known as the 'Trot o' Turra',[4] itself almost a proverbial phrase.

In the 1650s, there was some agitation about the Presbytery's conducting of school examinations,[5] but more exciting for the population in general was the burning of the Episcopal Chapel by a division of the Duke of Cumberland's army as it passed through in 1746 on its way to Culloden. The Chapel, at the corner of High Street and Main Street, was rebuilt in 1772 in Craigmyre Lane, which thereafter became known as Chapel Street.[6]

In general, however, an atmosphere of peace has been the keynote, as summed up in the words of Robert Southey, the Poet Laureate, on his visit to the town in 1819:

> Turriff stands prettily on a hill-side, and forms a pleasing picture in such a country, with a small stream at the bottom, a bridge and some bleaching grounds.
>
> The country round is broken in such a manner that ornamental culture might make it very beautiful. The town or village itself more straggling than Old Meldrum, but larger: it had one kirk in ruins, the best one which is in use stands in a kitchen garden. The best house in the place is a lawyer's—proof how this profession flourishes in Scotland. Watchmakers, as well as booksellers, seem much more numerous than in England: there are three in this little place.[7]

The small stream now has the uncomplimentary local name of 'the Gassie Burn', because it flowed past the gas works set up after the Gas Company was formed in 1840. There has been a great extension of new, white-walled housing, some of it to cater for farmers who have for some time had the habit of retiring into the town. The red-sandstone building that was Turriff Secondary School in my time there has been replaced by another in modern materials, and the School has become dignified by the name of Academy (keeping up, rightly, with Inverurie). One of Turriff's finest buildings in red stone, Erroll Lodging, was sadly demolished in the 1970s to improve access. The Central Auction Mart still stands, and it is to be hoped that disuse of the 'Central' through centralisation of Mart activities at Thainstone near Inverurie, will not lead to the loss of its highly-distinctive and attractive red-sandstone façade. But with all these changes, the core of Turriff can be seen still more or less as Southey saw it, though without the busy traffic.

National Insurance and the Turra Coo

The story of the 'Turra Coo' is an example of popular reaction to a form of government legislation at an important period in the shaping of the welfare state. The early 1900s in Britain were years of growing self awareness amongst working people. This was the period of the beginnings of the breakthrough of the Labour Party. In 1906, no fewer than 29 Labour members were elected to Parliament. By 1910, there were 40, though at that time only two represented Scottish constituencies.[8] Though forming only a minority, their influence was nevertheless strong enough to persuade the Liberal Government to embrace radical issues, through which the needs of ordinary people were taken into account more positively than had ever happened before. One of the results was the passing of the National Insurance Acts, 1911 and 1913, and the National Health Insurance (Collection of Contributions) Regulations (Scotland) 1913, which led to the disturbances that are discussed here.

The Acts were national in their application. In Scotland, the legislation was administered by the Scottish Insurance Commissioners, set up in 1911. They were answerable to the Treasury in London, and operated through local committees.

In essence, the Acts made insurance compulsory for the less well off employed workers between the ages of 16 and a maximum of 70, contributions being made by both worker and employer. The role of the State, using income from contributions, was to provide social welfare benefits such as medical services, sanatoria, maternity benefits, and payments during sickness or disablement. The normal rate of contribution in Britain was 7*d.* per week, of which the employer paid 3*d.* and the worker 4*d.* In practice the system was operated through National Health Insurance stamps which were bought and fixed onto cards, week by week. If the employer bought the stamps, he could reclaim his employees' contributions, e.g. by deduction from wages, but he was not allowed to reclaim the amount he was obliged by law to pay himself.

Though the Act marked a major advance in social welfare provision, in the early stages it was partial and imperfect, providing no help, for example, for people like the crofters of Highland Scotland who were deemed to be self employed, though they were low earners. It was actively disliked by many in Lowland rural areas because neither employer nor employed wanted to pay good money for stamps, for benefits the workers might never see; for the countryside view was that ill health was rarer there than in the towns and at that period unemployment was not a rural problem. Robert Barclay, farm servant, tailor and postman at different periods of his life in the neighbouring parishes of Forgue and Auchterless, made the point in the 1920s:

> I paid the National Insurance contributions from its commencement till I was 70, but never required doctor nor drugs, . . . I also for a short time paid the unemployment contributions, which does not merit my full approval like the National Health Insurance Act. I sympathise with those out of work, more so those with families, but young, strong, able-bodied fellows ought to have provision made for the proverbial 'rainy day' (i.e. through savings), and so be independent of the dole.[9]

If the worst came to the worst and it became necessary to join the dole queue, there was a strong feeling that this was degrading. No one liked to 'go on the b'roo'. In any case, help was given only if a minimum of 12 contributions had been paid, and then only for 15 weeks in any one year. It was also necessary for the dole candidate to prove that, though capable of work, he had genuinely been unable to find any.

When the Act was still a Bill under consideration by Parliament in 1911, there had already been widespread opposition to it. Leaflets were circulated against it.[10] In North-East Scotland, protest meetings began.[11] In December 1911, employees met in protest in Aberdeen and doctors in the town threatened to go on strike against the scheme. Several other meetings took place in 1912, but were ignored, and the Bill became an Act with full force of law. The Turriff District Protest Association was formed under the Secretaryship of Robert Paterson, farmer at nearby Lendrum, who is a main actor in the present story. On 23 August 1912, he issued a notice:

> The Committee have resolved to hold a Mass Meeting on Saturday, 31st inst, at Three P.M., within Johnston and Patersons Mart, and they strongly recommend that a General Half-Holiday be observed on that day, so that you and any of your Employees who are in sympathy with the protest may attend the Meeting.

Here, employers were taking the initiative in fostering solidarity with the employed.

About the same time, effigies of the Chancellor of the Exchequer, Lloyd George and of W H Cowan, the local Member of Parliament, were burned in the nearby town of Inverurie, and there was a protest meeting in Ellon, a little further off.[12] Popular feeling was clearly running high.

Further south, farmers were also refusing to pay insurance contributions. John B Kinnear in Fife was tried in the High Court of Justiciary on 6 June 1914 for failing to pay contributions for his grieve at Kinloch Home Farm, Ladybank, and a farm servant who lived at Trafalgar Cottages, Collessie. In Perthshire, William Sutherland at The Peel, Tibbermore, was pursued by the Scottish Insurance Commissioners from December 1912 for failing to pay insurance contributions of £24.16s.6d. for 14 employees. He was obliged to pay, though Sheriff Sym displayed obvious sympathy for 'a man who boldly sets at defiance a law of which he strongly disapproved, and was prepared to face the music and take the consequences'.[13]

But Sutherland did not rest. He set about organising a petition against the Act, 'to be signed by farmers, farm servants, and other electors pledging themselves to vote only for a Parliamentary candidate who, in turn, pledges himself to vote for the repeal of the Insurance Act as far as farm workers are concerned'. This 'Sutherland' movement was said to have spread all over the country, with widespread signing of petitions. Unionist candidates not pledging opposition were in danger of 'utter rout, so far at least as the rural constituencies are concerned'. The Sutherland petition, though demanding repeal of the Insurance Act, also pledged farmers 'to accept legal, instead of, as previously, moral responsibility only for their workers during sickness'.

The Lanarkshire Agricultural Society, like the Perth Agricultural Society, rounded up signatures; James Kidd, the Unionist candidate for Linlithgowshire, offered to vote for repeal of the Act; William Young, Liberal member for East Perthshire, told some farmers in his constituency that 'if they got a petition signed against the Act appealing to Mr Lloyd George to make it optional so far as farm workers are concerned, he would support them'. He was hedging his bets, and there was, in fact, a feeling that petition-signing was something of a farce. Pressure on Parliamentary candidates was thought likely to be more effective in achieving what the rural community, 'employers and employed alike for their interests are the same', wanted.[14]

Such cases got publicity at the time in the papers, yet they had no lasting impact on folk memory. There was no supporting cast such as there was in the case of the Turra Coo, to make the drama of the moment memorable.

Robert Paterson and the Work Force at Lendrum

The disturbances in Turriff, now to be described, were sparked off when Robert Paterson, of the nearby farm of Lendrum, refused to pay insurance stamps for his men. As an active Unionist, he was politically aware, and seems to have made his gesture in a carefully considered way, feeling that he was acting as much for the workers as for the farmers. His point of view, echoing that of Robert Barclay, quoted earlier, was that rural workers should not pay as much as industrial workers, since their conditions were so greatly different. He sought the agreement of his men. His daughter, Miss Elspeth B Paterson, has commented on the feeling of seriousness about the occasion when her father took each of the men separately into a room to explain that he was not going to pay the insurance stamps, and asked agreement from each not to do so. She can remember the sound of their feet at a time which must have seemed solemn. None of them appears to have objected. Miss Paterson's memory is supported by that of a Turriff man, William P Davidson, who later moved to California. He wrote to the *Turriff and District Advertiser* in 1971 that Paterson 'asked his employees if they wanted to pay the Insurance. They said "No". So Robbie said, "Alright we will not pay" '. This is how Davidson heard the story. He was 14 years old at the time.[15] The work-force at Lendrum then consisted of the grieve, foreman, second and third horsemen, orraman, bailie or cattleman, little bailie, a milkman (supplemented by milk boys hired in Turriff for a few hours, and who often came to Lendrum on Saturdays as a treat, between morning and evening deliveries), a cook, and a housemaid. All were 'kitchied', i.e. they had their meals in the kitchen. It was a big place for the district, of 330 acres.

According to one source, a cattleman called J G Scott presented his card for stamping. Robert Paterson accepted it, but next morning is said to have offered Scott the choice of staying till the end of his fee for a pound less than he had contracted for, or of going. The cattleman left. However, he was at once re-engaged on the neighbouring farm of Lescraigie, being paid for the remaining five weeks of the term as much as he would have had for six weeks

4

1 Back, left to right: Claude Forsyth (later Secretary of the RSPCC), William Morrice the grieve, a soldier, Alex and Jim Morrice, brothers.

Front, left to right: A soldier, Miss Alfrida F Paterson, Miss Lillian Paterson now Mrs A Hunter, Miss Margaret Paterson now Mrs F Hunter, Maggie Keir the maid, who later married Jock Riddoch, Lendrum Smiddy, Miss Elspeth B Paterson, a soldier, George Paterson (seated).

2 Some of the folk at Lendrum. Back, left to right: William Morrice, little bailie, servant lassie later Mrs J Mair, Robert Paterson, servant lassie Bella, Bertie Reid the milk cart laddie, Jim Morrice. Front, left to right: John Mair bailie, J G Scott, George Paterson, Alex Morrice, John Craib deaf and dumb horseman.

3   Jim Rennie on the Paterson's Dairy milk cart, about 1912. It made two journeys
a day into Turriff.

at Lendrum. Scott claimed that Paterson had arranged this in advance with his friend, Mr Park. All the same, when the trial took place later in Aberdeen, in January 1914, Robert Paterson said he did not stamp the cards of servants who had refused to present them, and that he did stamp the cards of those who brought them to him.[16] The name of Scott was not mentioned at the trial.

If the story is correct, as it seems to be, there could have been a good reason for Scott's involvement in this way. He was a member of the Turriff District Branch of the Farm Servants' Union, of which Turriff is considered to be the birthplace, at the time when James Kelman (at 6 Rae Street and later at 4 Wilson Lane) was its Secretary.[17] There was evidently some Union activity at the period among the farm servants of the district. It appears that the

Union was at first united with the farmers in opposing the National Insurance Act. As was said in an open letter to Lloyd George in the Union's Journal:

> It may seem very ungrateful of us, but your favourite child (i.e. the Act) is not popular amongst us. We don't like being hustled with things we have not been consulted about.[18]

At the very least there is a strong likelihood that Scott's involvement was known to his Union Branch. He seems to have sparked off the whole action, though whether he was a willing victim or a man caught in the middle is not entirely clear.

The Poinding of the Coo and its attempted Sale

Since Robert Paterson did not stamp his men's cards, he was charged on 14 August 1913 by the Procurator-Fiscal for failure to pay contributions under the 1911 National Insurance Act, in respect of persons in his employ. At a trial on 15 September, he was convicted and fined £15 for a total of 20 offences, valued at 15s. each. The Sheriff-Substitute then ordered a payment of £3.19s.10d. to the Scottish Insurance Commissioners as arrears of the contributions he should have paid under Section 69(2) of the Act. Paterson paid the fine, but objected to paying the arrears, the chief ground being that 'the order was pronounced without any due notice to him that it would or might be granted against him in the event of his conviction'. He complained of the intervention of the Commissioners, who were held not to have power to prosecute, of the Sheriff-Substitute's having refused to hear him on the subject of the Order, and of the Order's being inaccurate in amount (in fact by this time he should have been paying nearly £5, but the error was allowed to stand in his favour). His complaints were judged to be irrelevant, but he still refused to pay. There followed, as the documents put it, 'diligence thereon at the instance of Commissioners, including a poinding and sale', i.e. goods of appropriate value should be taken from the farm and sold to cover the arrears of what was due to the Commissioners. The poinding was authorised on 13 November 1913.[19]

An element of tragi-comedy then began to appear. George Keith, the Sheriff-Officer in Turriff, went to Lendrum to poind something of the value of £7, and chose a horned, white cow, a small-boned Ayrshire-Shorthorn cross, kept to serve the household with milk. Though Robert Paterson had a dairy herd with which he supplied milk to the town of Turriff, the dairy cows were worth more than was needed. No one would lend transport, so the cow, now immortalised as the 'Turra Coo' was led on foot to the town. Her sale was advertised for noon on Tuesday, 9 December 1913, in the Market Square at the head of the town, since neither of the two cattle Marts in Turriff, the Central and Johnston and Paterson's (Robert Paterson was a partner with Mr Johnston of Fraserburgh here), would sell her. Nor would either Mart provide an auctioneer for the sale, and a special licence was

4   Robert Paterson with the Turra Coo. From the *North British Agriculturist,* 11 December 1913.

required to bring Sammie S Gordon by train from the coastal town of Macduff to do the deed.

The occasion brought forth both popular slogans and crude verse. Before the white cow left the farm, Paterson took green paint and adorned her flanks with the words 'LG (i.e. Lloyd George) and Coo, Lendrum to Leeks' (with reference to the leek as the national symbol of Wales, the country from which Lloyd George came), and 'One Other Victim'. A rough sketch of an Insurance stamp was drawn on her hindquarters. This was seen by Paterson as a piece of sarcasm at the National Insurance Commissioners, whom he expected to become owners of the cow since he understood nobody intended to buy her at the sale. [20]

On the day of the sale, a placard was put up in the town, with words purporting to come in part from the lips of the cow:

'You have been sold;'
'I'm to be sold?'
'Ay, you've been sold!'
'And a victim I'm to be too,
Sold by command of the Sheriff, no less,
To keep up a beggarly crew
Of Insurance sharks
And a Welshman's tools,
A desperate thieving lot,
To rob the poor of their 4d a week,
To keep boiling a fraudulent pot.
Come then to the Square in your thousands,
From the laws grip set me free,
Back Lendrum up—
He deserves your aid
And get a good home for me.'[21]

As noon approached, a crowd estimated at 1,500 to 2,000 or more packed into the Square, farmers and men alike in their day-out clothes, complete with bonnets on their heads, and hands as often as not in trouser pockets.

The workers had been given a half holiday, which in itself is significant. A regular half holiday was one of the things the Scottish Farm Servants' Union had been fighting for, and on this occasion the farmers seemed to be willing to cooperate. Later the Union was to complain that:

> For the past year, Turra has been giving all its attention to resistance to the Insurance Act, and the men have been more interested in the fun of that than in promoting their own interests. The farmers have been willing to give half holidays to allow the men to gather and help them in the game they are playing.[22]

Obviously, even if the Union opposed the Act, it was not prepared to support the farmers. It considered the Turra Coo incident a 'political dodge by Tory farmers'.[23] Later, *The Scottish Farm Servant* was to note with much satisfaction in its pages that when the district was going wild about the 'White Coo', and the farmers were bent on making trouble for the visiting MP, Mr Cowan, the Turriff Branch took advantage of the MP's presence to tackle him about the half-day off, and got an apparently sympathetic hearing. As Mr Cowan said, though the farmers argued that a half holiday should not be given, yet 'on the occasions when they wanted to make a demonstration either at selling a White Coo, or presenting a White Coo, or

5, 6 The Coo on her way to be sold in the Square, Turriff, 9 December 1913.

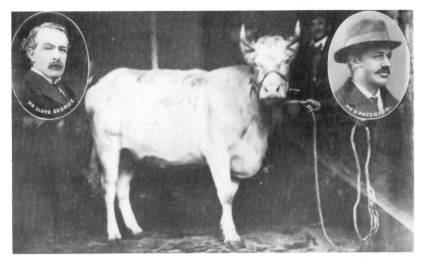

7   Probably the best-known postcard sold at the time, with the Coo in the middle
     flanked by vignettes of Lloyd George and Robert Paterson.

misbehaving at a political meeting, they have always managed to give a half
holiday to their men, in the hope that the latter would play the game'.[24] The
Union's Journal reported that farmers had been much disgusted when the
men promoted a movement of their own and persuaded Mr Cowan to
support them. No wonder, therefore, that it could tell an anti-farmer story
with glee:

> Turra is chuckling over a little episode in connection with the famous Turra Coo
> presentation. At one farm in the district, everybody left the place on that day to
> attend the splore in the town. A notice was stuck up on the kitchen door for the
> postie, telling him to put the letters in the washing house. This, by the way, by
> one of the farmers who was very strong against the half-holiday, and asserted
> that it would never do to have all the men away from the place at once.[25]

So the Union mocked the white cow, and the farmers, and the farm
servants who let the cow distract their attention from what the Union
officers saw as more basic issues. Though these were real and serious
enough, yet it can hardly be doubted that the day of the sale was a day of fun
as well as of disturbance. Turriff had never seen such an assembly. A passing

stranger, asking what was wrong, was told, true to the North-East humour: 'A mannie ca'd Robbie Paiterson wis to be hanged.' Several schoolchildren played truant that day. Girls were punished by writing out lines, and boys got six of the best with the strap.

When the cow appeared in the Square, three cheers were called for the 'Fite Coo'. She was in no mood to appreciate them, for when she was in Davidson the Painter's shed the night before, someone had tried to clean off the slogans on her sides with turpentine. White cows have tender hides and this alone, allied with the noise of the crowd, could scarcely fail to upset her. She arrived punctually in the Square, led by a boy who had a grip on her rope, but he had 'aneuch adoo wi'it'.[26]

There are vivid, if somewhat muddled, reports of what happened. According to the Sheriff Officer, when he reached the Square, the crowd was 'howlin' oot o' them . . . they cam down upon us, an' swypit us clean aff the Square coo an' a' '. When he tried to sell the cow, someone cut the rope and she set off the way she had come. A Turriff farmer, William Smart, claimed that he was in the act of examining the cow's mouth with a view to buying her (according to the local saying, 'a coo's aye a coo be the moo'), when she suddenly turned and made off, with a dog following her of its own free will.

Another witness, John Emslie, farmer in Monquhitter, said a dog was jumping about the cow and barking at her.[27]

Robert Paterson himself had not intended to be present. He had been busy selling stock in the Mart that day, but towards midday it became deserted and he was asked to delay the sale for half-an-hour. He went to the Square, but later denied that he shouted 'Hoo! hoo!', in the way people do to turn an agitated animal. In fact he seems to have tried to keep the cow in the Square, though he thought there were not enough attendants to keep the crowd from closing in on her.[28]

The point was important to Paterson, for after the legal proceedings had ended, he sent a letter to the newspapers on 10 June 1914, thanking his supporters and explaining what he claimed to be the root cause of the disturbance as it developed:

> In connection with this case we feel that, though in a sense we regret the necessity, we owe it to many friends who have stood loyally by us to make known an aspect of the case which has but recently come to light. In this disclosure the unbiased mind will perceive the real cause of the deforcement. When the poinded animal reached Turriff about half an hour before the time fixed for the sale, she was taken to the Sheriff Officer's stable, and there vigorously rubbed with turpentine to remove the inscription painted on her body. The lettering

having been put on the evening before was slow to respond. The turpentine gave out. A printer was called in with a fresh supply of the fluid, and the rubbing was renewed. Whether the real object was to obliterate 'Leeks' or 'Lendrum' or the 'Insurance Stamp' on the cow would be rather interesting to know. At any rate, the turpentine was applied on the living animal as if it had been a barn door. It is well known that turpentine has a most irritating effect upon animals, and on a white one even more than on a coloured one, because the hair is much thinner. By the time the cow reached the Square the effect of the treatment would have been at its height, and when the people pressed about her she would have become wild with pain, and had not she and the boy and the rope parted company it is hard to see how a nasty accident could have been averted. Had this circumstance been disclosed at the proper time it is highly improbable that any prosecutions would have taken place. . . .

This seems reasonable, though the writer does not actually express regret for the consequences (see Reference 44).

When the cow ran off, the crowd, then in humoursome mood,—as John Emslie said, 'everybody . . . was grand pleased with themselves'—turned to the auctioneer, Sammie Gordon, as a focus of attention. Fireworks were let off, bags of soot, eggs, kail stalks and other missiles were thrown. Gordon took refuge in a stable, where someone backed a horse into the stall where he was taking refuge, forcing him to scramble onto the manger. There were various shouts: 'Lock the door and keep him in!' and 'Come out and sell the cow and not show the white feather' but he was not hurt. In folk memory, farm people still relate that 'an antrin cloddie an a kail runt wis thrown'. One eye-witness was William Davidson, later of California, but then a grocer's assistant with Stewart the Baker. He noted three policemen from Turriff and two from King Edward. One was Inspector Copland and another Police Sergeant Scott, who was struck full in the face by a raw egg, to the great delight of the crowd, especially since the policeman in front of him ducked just in time. The auctioneer was finally led to the Sheriff's office, where the five policemen lined up and asked the crowd to move on.

The cow is said to have ended up in Hutcheon's Close, or else it went along Duff Street to Cheyne's barn, later to be Bertie Reid's Auction Rooms, where she was tied up. At any rate, she eventually got back to Lendrum with the kindly help of the milkman, John Mair.

The cow remained for three days at Lendrum, when she was again removed and taken by the Great North of Scotland Railway to Aberdeen. A second warrant of sale was taken out. It was to take place on premises at 8 Lower Denburn, Aberdeen, at 11 a.m. on Tuesday, 16 December, as advertised in the *Aberdeen Daily Free Press* and in the *Aberdeen Daily Journal* (in both cases only the day before), and as passed on to Robert Paterson by registered post. Meantime the cow was kept at a private stable belonging to Alexander Craig, Saddler and Harness Maker, at 53 and 55 Schoolhill. At the sale itself the public crowding around were excluded by order of the defenders (the Scottish Insurance Commissioners), and the auction proceeded with David R Hendry as auctioneer and James Conner, Sheriff Clerk Depute, as Judge of Roup. In the event, Alex Craig bought the cow for £7; he did well, for three days later he sold it to James Davidson for £14.[29]

The costs[30] of carrying out the sale were as follows:

Proceeds of sale		
Principal sum in decree	£ 3.10. 0	
Charging decree	0. 8. 5	
Poinding	0.13. 5	
To intimating sale	0. 8.10	
To paid George Keith for sale at Turriff	1. 8. 8	
To paid Sam S Gordon do.	1. 0. 0	
To paid Wordie & Co for removal of cow	0. 4. 0	
To paid G N of S Railway for carriage of cow	0.12.11	
To paid advertising sale at *Aberdeen Free Press* 4s; *Aberdeen Journal*, 3s.6d.	0. 7. 6	
To paid Alex Craig for keep of cow	1. 1. 0	
To paid D R Hendry, Auctioneer, Aberdeen	1. 1. 0	
To paid Judge of Roup his fee	0.12. 6	
	£11. 8. 3	£7. 0. 0

It takes little mathematical ingenuity to work out that there was a balance of £4.8s.3d. which it fell to the defender, the Scottish Insurance Commissioners, to pay.

On 24 December 1913, charges were brought against eight persons alleged to be implicated in the deforcement of the Sheriff Officer at Turriff. They pleaded not guilty, and the case was adjourned till 6 January 1914, for proof.[31] From 6 to 10 January 1914, the eight men were tried before Sheriff

8   Crowds at the sale of the Coo in Aberdeen, 16 December 1913.

Principal J Campbell Lorimer at Aberdeen, for Breach of the Peace and Deforcement of the Sheriff Officer.[32] The accused were: Robert Paterson, Lendrum; James Fullerton, his farm grieve; George Anderson, farmer, Drachlaw, Inverkeithny; George Bruce, farmer, Luncarty; Nathaniel Milne, auction mart attendant, Turriff; John Moir, farm servant, Little Colp; William Fraser, farm servant, Lenshie and George Davidson, farmer, Boghead, Dunlugas. Of these, Paterson, Fullerton, Anderson and Bruce were accused of deforcing the sheriff officer, and committing a breach of the peace; the others were charged with disorderly conduct and committing a breach of the peace. All pleaded not guilty. In the course of the six day trial, 33 witnesses for the defence were called. One of these said he regarded the Turra Coo incident 'as a mixture of joviality and ignorance'. In fact, the trial itself was not lacking in joviality either.

The decision given on the last day, Saturday, was 'not proven', a verdict received with applause in Court. 'In giving his decision the Sheriff said the first charge was one of deforcement of the Sheriff Officer against Paterson, Fullerton, Anderson, and Bruce. He didn't think it had been proved. It had rather been proved, although it was not necessary for him to come to any absolute conclusion upon it, that the only thing Paterson did was to endeavour to turn the cow back to the square and not to drive it away. His judgement therefore, on that charge was in favour of the accused. He did not think it proved that Fullerton hounded the dog against the cow. It was not established that there was a breach of the peace at the square. The third charge was the one about which he had the most difficulty. It was a charge of breach of the peace in regard to the auctioneer. The auctioneer seemed to have been a timid man, and went along the street to take refuge from the crowd, and went into a stable. Going along the street and in the stable things were done that constituted a breach of the peace, but for what happened the accused were not responsible. He, therefore, found all the charges not proven.'

After the trial, Paterson and his grieve took the train to Auchterless Station, where a large crowd was waiting to receive them. The others were also met by large crowds at Turriff Station, and a procession headed by pipers marched through the town, to the accompaniment of welcoming cheers. [33]

There is no doubt that Robert Paterson had widespread support. Archibald Campbell, Mains of Auchmunziel, New Deer, wrote on 16 January 1914 to Mrs Paterson to say he wanted to do a sketch of her husband for a forthcoming issue of the *Aberdeen Journal*. 'I will cycle up some evening and see you or both of you if possible. I am afraid some one else will get before me and steal my privilege. We are all delighted with Turriff and the organisation against a rotten act. I have done what I could but my support has dwindled away. Will you kindly grant me this interview?' Two days before Campbell wrote, there had been an ovation by Fraserburgh to Robert Paterson.

He had also become something of a national figure, to judge by a telegram sent from London by the *Daily Mail*, asking if Robert Paterson had got his cow back and what he intended doing in future regarding the Insurance Tax. He was—in a way more reminiscent of the parsimony generally held to be Scottish—asked to answer in 48 reply paid words. There is no record that he did so.

The Return of the Cow

The legal sources do not identify the James Davidson who bought the cow for £14 other than through his name on the receipt given by Craig. He appears to have been James Davidson, Mill of Rora, Longside. He fetched the cow back to Turriff, after a number of Buchan farmers had clubbed together to cover the cost, on 20 January 1914. The prime-mover seems to have been Alex Watson, Whitehills, Gamrie, a cattle dealer. When Alec Winton erected a monument to the Coo at Lendrum many years later in 1971, he got a letter from William Black, Estate Manager, Tillypronie Estates Ltd, that proved this point:

> I had a small part in the return of the Turra Coo to Robbie. The late Alex Watson, Whitehills, Gamrie (cattle dealer) was collecting for the Price of the Cow when I as a laddie of 10 years led the Coo round the Hill of Pitgair and as far as Mill of Minonie, where Mr Watson's brother Wm Watson was farmer & Millar. I lived at Hill of Bush at that time.[34]

The return of the wanderer gave rise to a second large gathering, attended by the Coo which again bore slogans: 'Free!! Divn't ye wish that ye were me', and 'Breath Bad—Gummy Leeks', in reference to Lloyd George and the national emblem of Wales. She entered the Market Square in procession, headed by the band playing 'See the Conquering Hero Comes'.

According to a report of the period, the ceremony of the Coo's return took place in a field adjoining the Market Square. 'Rarely has Turriff seen such a crowd . . . to compute the numbers at between 3,000 and 4,000 persons is by no means an over-estimate.' Many women were present, which had not been so at the attempted sale earlier. Soon after 1.30 p.m. the cow appeared from the mart gates, 'in all the glory of vari-coloured ribbons, and bedecked with "everlasting" flowers on her branks and neck-chains . . . Crowds lined Balmellie Street and Main Street as the procession stepped towards the park and from the windows of the houses on each side of the street there was a perfect medley of white and coloured handkerchiefs waved in enthusiastic greeting to the great "white coo" . . . The speeches of Mr Campbell and Mr Paterson, in reply, were punctuated with firework interruptions, but both

19

9   The Coo returning to Turriff to be presented back to Robert Paterson, 20 January
1914. Postcard by 'Dunn, Photographer, Brechin'.

gentlemen waited good humouredly until the temporary turmoil had
subsided.'

Archibald Campbell, Mains of Auchmunziel, made the presentation
speech. He praised 'the hero of the hour, Mr Paterson . . . the way he has all
along, with a few more stalwarts about Turriff, shown up the injustices of the
parasitical Insurance Act, at once proclaims him as a leader among men.
(Cheers) . . . the Insurance Act is the most contemptible effort of modern
times by the "powers that be" to levy a tax on the important industry of
agriculture, to support a myriad of undesirable and improvident mechanical
operatives in our large cities . . . let me present to you the "Turra Coo",
returned by an overwhelming majority from "Leeks to Lendrum" (Laughter
and cheers, and a Voice "Three cheers for Robbie").'

Robert Paterson made a reply, accepting the Coo. 'I . . . accept her for
return to her natural home at Lendrum, as being really the natural place for
her. (Cheers, and a voice—"Pit her in the same sta") . . . The telegrams of
congratulation and the letters and post-cards that have been pouring in, not

10, 11 Crowds in Turriff at the presentation of the Coo in the 'Market Parkie'. The men all wear bonnets. Postcards by 'Dunn, Photographer, Brechin'.

12   Those attending the presentation wore their best clothes for the occasion. A 'Holmes' Silver City Series Postcard'.

13   The brass band increased the festival atmosphere at the presentation of the Coo

only to myself, but to the other seven who were tried for the deforcement of the Sheriff Officer in Turriff, have shown to us the widespread and deep interest that has been taken in the matter. (Cheers) I can assure you my feelings are that it was not because the people abroad thought the people of Turriff were guilty of any direct infringement of the law, or any disrespect to the officers of the law, but they did not wish to show how the ripple of laughter had spread, not only over the district, but over the larger parts of Scotland. (Cheers) What they did wish . . . was an incident by which they could show their antipathy to the Insurance Act. (Cheers) . . . I would point out the meaning of these incidents taking place in Turriff. (Cheers) Our people being free born, and having that sense of liberty that has always been a pride to us, as British citizens—(hear, hear)—we will rouse up and show them that we will not have their dictation. (Hear, hear and cheers) . . . I say, under our constitution, we have the liberty and the right to take such constitutional means as we may to protest against that Act. . . .'

The crowd dispersed as the band played a medley of Scottish tunes after the speeches. There was no trouble, though Inspector Copland of Inverurie's force of 20 sergeants and constables was standing by. Justice had been done, in the popular view, and it was a gala occasion.[35]

Other North-East Cases

Robert Paterson's refusal to conform to the law was not unique in the North-East. A Committee Meeting of the Turriff District Protest Association (of which Paterson was Secretary) in October 1913 took notice of the treatment of three farm servants recently sentenced in Aberdeen for contravention of the Act. They were George McLeod, George Grant and George Michie, servants to Mr Walker, farmer, Birkenhills, Turriff, who pleaded guilty to a charge of having failed to apply to an approved society or to a postmaster for a contribution card. Rather than pay the fines they were given, they chose prison, though the fines were found for them and they were let out after three days.

The Secretary told the Meeting of the men's poor treatment in prison. 'As an association,' he said, 'they were not to take matters humbly. . . . They had . . . received letters complimenting them on the stand they had made in opposing such a detestable Act.' Five of their members had been summoned between August and October, and four had paid penalties. The sentences seemed more harsh than any given elsewhere in Scotland, perhaps in retaliation for the stiffness and determination of the opposition in Turriff. Mr Paterson said 'many men were presenting their cards simply because they were terrified. There were dozens in the district, however, who would not get cards.' It was thought by Mr Walker that the men were doing more to resist than the farmers. [36]

Another local farmer who fell in with the atmosphere of the time was Alexander Duncan, farmer at Penelopefield, Forglen, who for a 20 week period from 12 January till 28 May 1914, failed to pay his contribution in respect of James Reid, Boghead, Haddow, Inverkeithny, whom he employed as a farm-servant at Burnend Farm, Carnoustie, Forglen, at a rate of wages exceeding 2s. per working day, and to whom he paid wages in respect of employment about the time of the May term, to use the legal jargon.

According to the Insurance Commissioner's solicitor, the farmer 'engaged James Reid on the understanding that he was to have certain allowances, such as a house, potatoes, and to be allowed to keep a cow, while he was also to have a fixed sum of about £28 in wages. When engaging him, accused,

24

he alleged, informed Reid that if any inspector under the Insurance Act came round he was to say he got no wages. At Whitsunday 1914 accused told Reid he would not pay him any wages unless and until he signed a document to the effect that he had been with him learning farming, and was obtaining no pay, and that he had no claim on him when he left. In order to get payment of his wages, Reid signed the document. This was an attempt to appear to come under a section of the Act that allowed exemption from compulsory insurance. Duncan pleaded guilty, and was fined £5 by Sheriff Dudley Stuart at Banff for his earnest endeavour to find a loophole.'[37]

Robert Paterson, therefore, was not the only one, though it is evident that he played a stimulating role that undoubtedly had knock-on effects.

Aftermath

With the return of the white cow to Lendrum, a stage was ended, but the story was not yet over. Robert Paterson had sued the Scottish Insurance Commissioners for reduction (annulment) of a minute for them as defenders in a complaint at the instance of the Procurator-Fiscal of Aberdeenshire; of an extract of an order granted by Sheriff-Substitute Laing in Aberdeen Sheriff Court ordaining that he should pay £3.19s.10d. of the execution of a charge following on the decree; and of the poinding proceeding on the extract and of the warrants of sale of the effects poinded. He claimed £250 in damages and £50 in expenses, partly on the grounds that his business had been affected. In proof of this he drew attention to the level of sales in Johnston and Paterson's Mart, and to his milk sales.

	Mart Sales		
	1912	1913	1914
Cattle	5339	5592	5422
Pigs	9159	7653	9788

Milk Sales from Lendrum			
1910–11	1911–12	1912–13	1913–14
£906.8.1	£914.3.9	£871.5.2	£827.7.8 [38]

Cattle sales did not support the contention, though pig sales certainly dropped in 1913. Milk, which was retailed twice daily, except on Sundays, from Lendrum's cart, did not sell so well in 1912–14. There was reduction of income, certainly, but it was not easy to blame this only, if at all, on National Insurance resistance. Though these points were submitted, Lord W J Cullen made no reference to them in his judgement.

The case for the pursuer, Robert Paterson, was therefore primarily based on other factors: that the proceedings relating to the obtaining of the order to pay arrears of £3.19s.10d. and the diligence thereon, were oppressive and lawless; that the defenders, the Commissioners, had shown an utter disregard of the ordinary rules of diligence, the poinding being grossly irregular through failure of the first attempt at a sale in Turriff and secrecy

26

in obtaining a warrant of sale on 13 December for the second sale in Aberdeen on 16 December, which was conducted with the public excluded, so that the cow fetched much less than its real value.

The defenders maintained that they had throughout acted in a perfectly legal manner, and under warrant of the Sheriff. Since the poinding was made necessary because of the pursuer's wilful refusal to pay a lawful debt, he was not entitled to damages. Nevertheless they offered to consent to decree of reduction of certain of the proceedings, and to pay £50 damages in settlement of the action.[39]

In the Outer House of the Court of Session, Lord Cullen 'found the averments of the pursuer irrelevant so far as directed to reduction of the minute and extract order by the Sheriff; sustained to that extent the defender's plea; and allowed both parties a proof, excluding, by consent of pursuer, the pursuer's averment as to his having been accused of deforcement and expense in defending himself against that charge'.[40]

The proof took place before the Lord Ordinary, without a jury, though Paterson had requested one. In the end, Lord Cullen's judgement was that he 'assoilzied (decided in favour of) the defenders from the conclusion of the summons relating to the minute and the order following upon it. He granted decree for reduction of the other documents and decree for payment to the pursuer of £39. In respect of a tender lodged by the defenders in February 1914 consenting to reduction and to £50, the defenders were found entitled to expenses since the date of the tender'[41] (which accounts for the reduction of the amount of expenses to £39).

Some details of Robert Paterson's visit to Edinburgh survive. He seems to have enjoyed his trip to the capital, where he stayed in the old Waverley Hotel, 43 Princes Street. He was invited to a function about which he wrote on 6 February to his wife Peggie:

> I have just returned from that famous function and although I had great scruples about going I am now really pleased I went.
> There were in all about 90 present and a very distinguished and a very successful gathering it was. I was introduced to very many people of standing who all knew me—and the cow by reputation. . . .
> Mr Forhuie met me at the Station and after we had something to eat went to the Court of Session where I was introduced to and made the acquaintance of many distinguished people in the legal profession and who also all seemed much interested in our case in Edinburgh and in our doings in the north. . . .
> My only difficulty was when I came to dress for that affair (I did not think it much of a difficulty). Mr F when I seemed reluctant to come hinted that a white

vest would make me feel all right so well I went and got one took it to Hotel and there found it just tight enough not a good arrangement for a big dinner—got it on and also a light tie which I did not know how properly to fix—got that all right, . . . and looked and felt pretty spry except for the rusty edge of a sticking through a cloth button on the most prominent part of my frock coat (I got it pressed in Aberdeen) but I made this all right by rubbing it with blake off one of my boots. Thus I appeared at, was much spoken about and enjoyed myself at this important dinner. I lost count of the courses and my rest was far too little.[42]

It was perhaps a reflection of this occasion, or of the case, that inspired the well-known natural historian, John A Harvie-Brown of Dunipace House, Stirlingshire, to write a jocular letter to a friend on 5 February, in Scots:

There's that Coo again! If it gangs aften thro' the midden-glaur, it'll come oot gie Ken-speckled! But go it, Mr Paterson! *Fifty* pun'!! What's that: only a flea i' the lug to '*the State*'—how many servant's *thrippences* & *fourpences* is that, to what Mr L L George has snappit up till *himsel' and his* £400—friends in Parliament?' (670 up @ £400 a piece), ma Conscience!! And wha's bearing the weight o' a' that, I'd like to ken. Aye, sic' a callant as he is!! and man! he's a nailer at quoting Scriptur.—

> Lloyd George na doubt,
> When Life ebbs oot,
> Will career in a flaming chariot,
> Or sit in state
> On a red-hot plate,
> 'Tween the Devil & Judas Iscariot.
> Ananias will say
> To the *Devil* that day,
> Our claim for pre-eminence fails;
> So sit up one higher;
> Keep away from the fire,
> And make room for that Liar from Wales!
> Hech!!'[43]

On 10 June 1914, Robert Paterson took to his pen to thank, in the columns of the press, those who had supported him:

Sir—Seeing that the final stage in the chain of incidents associated with what is familiarly known as the 'Turra Coo Trial' has been reached, namely the settlement of accounts connected with it, permit me . . . sincerely to thank all friends for their kind sympathy and congratulations, and not the least for the practical help extended to the eight men who underwent a long trial at Aberdeen Court for an alleged infringement of the law. To defend so many, necessarily entailed a great deal of professional labour. The heavy preparatory work, the engagement of five solicitors for practically a whole week in our defence, would have entailed a very serious drain on the resources of many of the accused. Realising this, and having the fullest sympathy with the cause we represented, the public came most generously to our aid with the result that the magnificent sum of £96.12s. was sent towards our expenses. These expenses amounted to an average of £18 for each of us—generous in their moderation we all thought— so the sum subscribed, not only entirely discharged the account of all the wage-earners, but materially helped to reduce the sum falling to the others. . . .[44]

Robert Paterson

To assess the Turra Coo case properly, it is necessary to look at 'Robbie Paiterson' in the context of his time. He was born in Turriff (Balmellie Street) on 11 August 1868, the youngest of a family of seven. His father's folk had been farmers around Buckie, and his father was for a time grieve at Lendrum, the farm Robert later took over.

Some of his business ability, at least, was inherited from his mother, Elspeth Brodie Paterson, who started the first dairy in Turriff. Night and morning the cows went from the byre at the back of the house through the town to the 'Allotted Lands' on the Haughs where the 'Turra Show' is now held every August, or to the 'Brodie Braes', now called 'the Den'. In May 1971, the 92 year old Catherine H Adams wrote from Oldmeldrum to say of Robert Paterson:

> I had known him as a boy as we were neighbours in Balmellie St. They flitted down to where the new garage is then they built the property where Mr Leonard has his Hiring Garage we flitted to Fife Street and I ran down the lanes for the milk before going to school in my mind's eye yet I can see Mrs or Robbie ladling out the milk which was only 1*d*. a pint they started with one cow & had 22 cows to go to Lendrum. So we were always friends Mother loved to go to a roup in the Mart he used to give her a bargain.
>
> I was on the Square where the crowd was for the sale of the cow, pour auctiner [sic] never got his word in he had to run for shelter even the policemen (could not) do anything but stay beside the man. So I often look back on those days glasses china etc. had the white coo on it at that time. Mr Paterson did a lot of good in his quiet way . . .[45]

As the letter indicates customers called with their pails for milk at first. Later, a pony and milk cart went round the town when Robert had developed the business at Lendrum after 1904. Albert (Bertie) A Reid, later, a well-known Turriff auctioneer, was a milk boy at Lendrum at the time of the Turra Coo, when he was 13 years old.

Robert cemented the floor of the Balmellie St byre and replaced the wooden travises between the cows with cement ones, marking a care for

14   A rare picture of James Paterson, father of Robert. He was born in 1815, the year
of the Battle of Waterloo, near Buckie. For a time he was grieve at Lendrum, with
Mr Henderson, farmer. His two other sons were James and Vermont. He died at
Turriff in 1898.

15   Robert Paterson's wife Margaret (Peggie) in 1913.

hygiene that was ahead of his time. When the business expanded and they rented Lendrum, he also showed a pioneering spirit by sterilising all the milk vessels by steam daily, using boilers bought from Macduff trawlers.

In 1902, his brother George in Liverpool[46] gave him the chance to visit the McDonald Agricultural College in Montreal, Canada. Since the Lendrum soil was in poor shape, he had samples analysed there, and thereafter ordered manures in exact quantities to suit his land. He bought them at Hutcheon's, Turriff, and had them mixed at Lendrum. Here, again, he was a pioneer in his district.

He took a keen interest in agricultural education, at a time when neither day nor evening classes were locally available. He was always happy to welcome any farmer, young or old, who was interested in improving methods of production. He paid fees for a grieve to attend evening classes in Aberdeen, and when living at Balquholly, he gave talks on woods and trees to lads who visited him with their teachers from Auchterless and other schools.

His business expansion started with the death of Mr Chapman, Meikle Hilton, who had a sawmill plant that Robert secured. During the First World War, he carried out a very successful business in the wood trade in Aberdeenshire, Ross-shire and Perthshire, even sending consignments of timber to France. He later purchased the estate of Delgaty and Greeness, Turriff; Arnage, Ellon; part of the Mounblairy Estate; and his later home at Balquhollie. The farms he ran, in addition to Lendrum, were the Home Farms of Delgaty and Aquhorthies, Idoch, Rosebrae, Haremoss, and Burnside of Mountblairy.

In an associated area of business, he was an auctioneer, valuator and partner in the privately owned Mart of Johnston and Paterson, in Balmellie Street, Turriff. Before this, he had gained experience by acting as clerk to John Bell of the Turriff Mart for a number of years. He was famous for his witty remarks at the roups where he officiated. This no doubt helped to make him a welcome speaker also at political meetings on behalf of the Unionist Party. He appeared on many platforms when Col Burn was contesting Aberdeenshire. He was much in demand for opening sales of work. As an ardent member of the Turriff Mutual Improvement Society, he also gave lectures, for example on 'The Progress of the World' in a number of local schools. He was active in the Young Men's Christian Association, and would cycle with his friends to Aberdeen to hear famous preachers like the revivalist American, Dwight Lyman Moody, and Ira D Sankey, the 'American Singing Pilgrim'. There was more than a passing interest here, for

16 Photograph of a painting of Robert Paterson, done in 1930 by Mrs Mitchell, Aberdeen College of Art.

17   Mrs A Massie feeding the hens at Lendrum, with Lilian Paterson and a friend in the background, in 1925.

18   Harvesting at Lendrum. One binder is pulled by a Titan tractor and the other by horses.

his wife Margaret (Peggie), whom he married in 1901 (and who had been at school with him), spent nine years in the USA where she graduated from Northfield Seminary, which Moody and Sankey had founded.

For 34 years, he was an elder of St Ninian's Kirk, and for long acted as superintendent of its Sunday School. When living at Lendrum, he conducted a Sunday School at Birkenhills, with the help of his wife, family and friends, and provided picnics at Balquhollie for the Sunday School scholars. He and other members of the Mutual Improvement Society and the YMCA held open meetings on Saturday evenings, with the intention of providing a pleasant meeting place for farm workers. Like many such well-intentioned efforts, this failed, since the men preferred to move around in freedom and 'have a news' with all whom they met.

When the minister, Rev Duncan McLaren, came on a visit to Lendrum, Robert Paterson would take him to the kitchen to talk to his men, the cook and the housemaid. This was an unheard of action at the time. The men were all fed in the kitchen, though they slept in a bothy.

It is significant that several families had two or more members in his employ for years, e.g. the families of Hendry, Paul, Paterson, Doig, Mutch, Johnston, Grant, Massie, Morris, at a time when single men tended to change masters every six months and married men every year. His paternalistic interest in his men had other proofs. James Reid, of Haremoss and later of Newton of Greeness, was interested in drawing. Robert arranged for Mrs Mitchell,[47] of the Aberdeen College of Art to give him lessons. He also gave financial help where men wanted to branch out on their own.

He was active in public life. He was a Town Councillor, and the Monquhitter Parish representative on the Turriff District Committee of Aberdeenshire. The Turra Coo affair in no way diminished his popularity, for on 18 April 1914, after it was over, he came top of the poll in the Turriff School Board election. He was a member of the Aberdeenshire Education Authority for 13 years.

His technical skills were also undoubted. He designed and organised the building of bridges to replace fords at Colp and Haremoss. The job was done at the slack time for farmers, between turnip hoeing and harvest. He also designed and built a grieve's house in timber at Lendrum, and a pavilion for the Den in Turriff, where his mother's cows had grazed, which he presented to the Turriff British Legion. He had a hand, too, in the designing of a naval gun.

With all this, he still found time to indulge in hobbies and pastimes. He was an accurate shot, for instance, and liked to collect unusual stones and

19   The men at Delgaty sawmill. Fifth from the left is George Paul.

20   A vehicle for hauling timber from the wood to the sawmill.

21   Robert Paterson at Balquhollie House in 1930. The woods around were bought
from the Tweeddales during the War.

walking sticks. Besides designing bridges and buildings, he carved a hall
chair, still owned by the family, with his wife's initials on the seat. He was
an active member of the Dramatic Society, a cricketer, and eventually
President of the Turriff Cricket Club.[48]

As farmer, milk retailer, auctioneer and valuator, livestock salesman,
timber merchant, contractor and public figure, Robert Paterson led a busy
life, in spite of earlier illness. However, he collapsed and died at the age of 67,
on 7 December 1934, in a restaurant in Aberdeen. Local papers carried

funeral reports listing the names of the large numbers of people present. His coffin was carried from church to hearse by overseers from his farms: James Cassie of Lendrum, David Milne of Greeness, William Shivas of Delgaty Home Farm, and William Morrison, of Brownhill of Mountblairy. The bearers for the next stage from hearse to grave in Turriff Churchyard (New Cemetery), were timber workers, George Paul, James Still, George Thain and Frank Robb.

The *Scotsman* also carried an Obituary, which took note of his opposition to the National Health Insurance Act, of his expanding business operations as a timber merchant, landowner and farmer, of his administrative skills in public work, and of his associations with the Mart. He was described as the most genial of men, who could also be a stout opponent.

All this was achieved by one who left school at 14, and who twice suffered bouts of rheumatic fever.

The obituary ended: 'Latterly, when any remark was made about what came to be known as the "Turra coo", he would smile and say, "That's a' bye noo".'

The Later Story

The matter is not 'a' bye'. Neither the man nor the moment have been forgotten, and the Coo lives on. Nearly 60 years after the event, Robert Paterson received a lasting tribute through the interest and generosity of Alex Winton, who had become farmer at Lendrum. In collaboration with the Paterson family, he planned and erected a fitting memorial at the entrance to the farm, with a well attended opening ceremony on 31 October 1971.

The stones at the top were collected from Robert Paterson's seven farms, and from the site of one of his sawmills, by his family. The white marble border was made from the Lendrum fireplace. It was built by Mr Duncan, Mason, Cuminestown, with three plaques inscribed by Ironside & Son, Stonecutters, New Deer. One plaque commemorates Robert Paterson, another the white cow, and the third Mr and Mrs Alex Winton. The dedication of the memorial was by the Rev Robert Barr, Auchterless.

There were several speakers: Professor Alan C Lendrum, Professor of Pathology at the University of Dundee; Harry J Sim, Kingsford, Auchterless, as Convener of the Landward Committee of the County Council; Patrick Wolrige-Gordon, MP; and Alex Winton himself. This was worthy public recognition. There was a further element of interest at the ceremony, for a tune by the composer Scott Skinner was played on a tape-recorder. This tune, which had been kept in unpublished form by the sister of Scott Skinner, was called 'The Turra Coo'.[49]

There can be no doubt that Robert Paterson was a man who was highly respected, not only locally, but also by those in Aberdeen and Edinburgh with whom he had dealings during the legal proceedings. As the Editor of *The Scottish Farm Servant* neatly put it:

> It is quite evident ... that local sympathy is with the resisters, and they have been getting such receptions that there is no doubt but they think themselves something of heroes.[50]

It is significant, in view of this background, that nowhere does *The Scottish Farm Servant* seek to make a villain of Robert Paterson, as a 'big farmer' ever

22   Alexander Winton speaking before the unveiling by Miss E B Paterson of the
Turra Coo Memorial.

anxious to make an extra penny at the expense of his work force. This is the
more extraordinary when it is remembered that in 1912, workers in this
very area had appealed to Joseph Duncan, then Chairman of the Aberdeen
Trades Council, for help in forming a union, largely because of growing
discontent over low wages and a very long working week, allied to the
stimulation caused by the strong opposition to the health insurance scheme,
with its weekly contributions from workers and employers. The workers
called a meeting at the same time as they wrote to Duncan, who read their
letter at a Trades Council meeting. The report in the *Aberdeen Journal*, 2

23 Presentations of flowers at the unveiling. Left to right: Miss Elspeth B Paterson, Mrs Margaret Hunter, Mrs Winton, Mrs G Paterson.

24   Some of the crowd at the unveiling.

THE OLD GAME.

THE LITTLE WELSH WONDER.—"Gentlemen, try these celebrated wind-spasm
pills of mine, compounded of the essence of rare and refreshing fruit,
guaranteed to cure land hunger, labour unrest, Turra cow-pox, and every
other ill. All you need is faith, my friends. Ninepenny boxes now
going for fourpence!" (Left talking).

25–27 Political cartoons of the period, ridiculing Lloyd George and also the farmers.
From *The Scottish Farm Servant*, 1913 and 1914.

THE ONLY WAY.

No one can be found in Aberdeen to sell the Turriff cow, which was poinded to meet the claims of the Insurance Commissioners against its owner.

Mr. FARMER FACING BOTH WAYS.

Mr. Farmer (to Mr. Lloyd George)—Nae need for an Insurance Act, ma mannie, for ploomen. We aye pay them their wages when they're sick.

Ditto (to Farm Servant)—Pay ye wages when ye're sick ! Na, fegs, ye have the Insurance Act noo.

February 1912, observed that: 'If any member of the Council had friends in the county, they might do what they could to encourage this organisation which had started in the Turriff district and was now spreading in a manner that was most hopeful.'

In fact it proved difficult to make much progress even in the Turriff area. This was partly due to extravagant demands by a minority, that the Union should seek an immediate 20 per cent wage increase. Duncan did not succeed in persuading them to be more reasonable. As far as fostering of opposition to the Health Insurance Act was concerned, local farmers persuaded their men to use meetings sponsored by the Union to oppose it.

28, 29 Two sides of a comic postcard sent to Mrs Paterson from Rothiemay on 9 February 1914.

Speakers at meetings wasted much time in explaining the value of the Insurance scheme, when they should have been trying to gain support for Union policies.[51]

The view of Paterson as an exploiter is more that of writers with Marxist approaches, who see men like Paterson as capitalist manipulators of workers, allied to those who 'organised peasant factions in defence of specific capitalist interests'.[52] This is how one academic has seen him, and also how James Leatham, who became provost of Turriff, saw him. At the time of the Turra Coo Case, Leatham lived in the North of England, running a printing press. He moved his press to Turriff during the First World War, and his views led him to print several articles over a period of years against Robert Paterson. Neither of these writers came from the Turriff area, or even from Scotland, and their knowledge of more urbanised and more industrialised conditions might have made it hard for them to appreciate the strength of rural community interest in districts like Turriff, which creates a kind of democracy of its own. The whole Turra Coo incident, a popular disturbance that was for most as much a chance for a bit of fun as an act of resistance to interfering officialdom, points straight to the nature of the tightly-knit community where it took place, and of comparable communities around it.

It has left concrete traces also: the memorial cairn; a number of effusions in verse; a long continuing series of press notices, not only the reports of the period, but also much later reminiscences and samples of reporting that will no doubt continue to appear like the phases of the moon; several postcard photographs were circulated; letter paper and envelopes bore the Turra Coo imprint; and as a motif on china and glass, as plates, saucers, ashets, mugs, tumblers and wall plaques, the Turra Coo is far from dead. Older pieces are now much sought after. It is not known where they were made, though the Bo'ness pottery is a possibility for some. One white, blue-rimmed shallow saucer in the possession of Alex Winton bears a crude, rectangular stamp in blue showing the cow alongside an inscription. It has a maker's mark on the back: 'E.P. Co., Empire Works, Stoke-on-Trent, England 18'. The stamp was no doubt added to a stock item. More recent enterprise by Peter's in the High Street, Turriff, has produced a mug and saucer, each adorned with the Coo and a group of bonneted men behind her, made by the 'Tom Raymond Pottery, England'. The Coo has even appeared as a pocket motif on young lady's aprons.

Besides all this, the Coo has found its way into the writings of historians and ethnologists. An American publication on *Edwardian Scotland* outlined the story in 1976,[53] and the present writer has published two articles.[54] The fact that one was reviewed in the *Observer Scotland* (19 March 1989) suggests that the affair still attracts national interest.

This popular disturbance, therefore, leaves its own literary and artistic record. Robert Paterson has become a folk-hero, though it is entirely typical of North-East humour that the Turra Coo herself outshines all in memory and myth.

Acknowledgement. I am grateful for a great deal of help from two of Robert Paterson's daughters, Miss L B Paterson and Miss A F Paterson, and also to Mr Alexander Winton, formerly farmer at Lendrum.

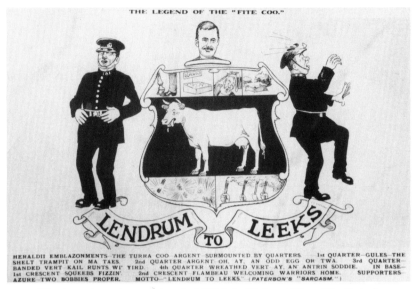

30   A comic cartoon postcard of 1913, in 'Holmes' Silver City Series'.

31   A comic Turra Coo cartoon from the *People's Journal*, 24 January 1914.

32   A Turra Coo bowl, in possession of G Cruickshank, Edinburgh.

33   A Turra Coo mug, in author's possession.

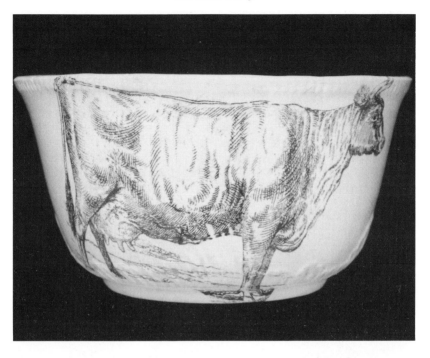

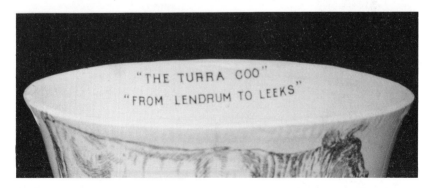

34, 35   A Turra Coo bowl, in possession of G Cruickshank, Edinburgh.

36   A Turra Coo plate, in author's possession.

37   A Turra Coo plate, in possession of G Cruickshank, Edinburgh.

38   A small Turra Coo ashet, in possession of the National Museums of Scotland.

39   A Turra Coo plate, in possession of G Cruickshank, Edinburgh.

40   A Turra Coo plate, in possession of G Cruickshank, Edinburgh.

41   A Turra Coo wall plaque, in possession of G Cruickshank, Edinburgh.

42 A modern Turra Coo mug and saucer, sold by Peters in Turriff, in author's possession.

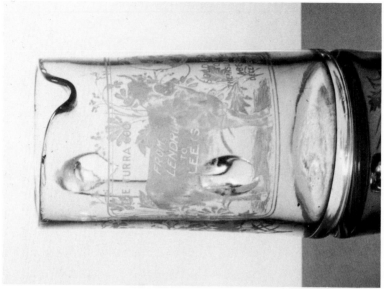

43, 44   A glass Turra Coo jug, in author's possession.

45, 46 A glass Turra Coo tumbler, in possession of G Cruickshank, Edinburgh.

47 A model of a cow with Turra Coo mottoes on its sides, with Alexander Winton, formerly farmer in Lendrum, who presented it to the National Museums of Scotland.

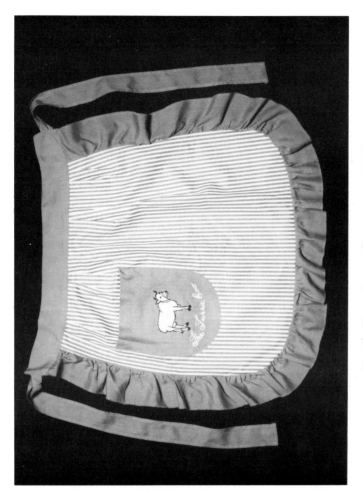

48   The Turra Coo motif on an apron, 1970s.

Appendices

1. The Fate of the Cow

The Turra Coo herself was bred by Patrick Smith at South Blachree and was sold to Macterry, Fyvie. She was a middling animal, not much of a milker even at her best, according to Mrs Nellie Josephs, 28 Broompark Crescent, Murthly, Perthshire, who, as a 13-year-old lass, started her working life at Bairnsdale, Fyvie, and then moved to Macterry, where as housemaid and then 'kitchie deem' she earned £4. 10s. in the half-year. There, she had to milk a white cow from Blachree. This was the one that gained so much fame after being sold to Lendrum.[55]

After her poinding and return to Lendrum, in the course of nature the cow bore a calf which was much pampered. In the true style of popular culture, people said the could see a '3d' and a '4d' on its sides, the amount of the Insurance Stamp contributions. But the calf died of anthrax and the carcase was burned.

After 6 years at Lendrum, the cow herself died. The vet, Mr Johnston, said that she had bovine tuberculosis, and blamed it on her enforced journeys, but after all, this disease was far from uncommon at that period. She was buried in a corner of a field, with sadness but without ceremony, and rested there till her bones were disturbed when Lendrum got an extra water supply.

2. The Dog that Chased the Cow

Details about the Cow incident are legion. It is an aspect of folk-memory that additional points come to light and are added to the story from time to time, not always accurately. There is also a desire to get in on the act. The Turra Coo case is no exception. When an article appears in a newspaper, there are responses, and the story grows. An example is a letter, undated, from Geordie Crighton, Crimond, to Alex Winton at Lendrum.

> I see your article in the Saturday Press & Journal about the Legend of the famous 'Turra Coo'. Well there has been a lot about her but never a word about the man and his dog that chased the coo. I am sending you this photo of them as I have

60

49   Mrs McLaren wife of the Minister of Turriff Church, with the Turra Coo at Lendrum in 1914.

50   The Rev D McLaren, Turriff, and Mrs Spottiswood, Muiresk, with the Turra Coo
at Lendrum in 1914.

51 The Turra Coo with Miss E B Paterson and Lilian (right), Miss Spottiswood of Muiresk House, the Rev D and Mrs McLaren, Mrs Paterson and Margaret Paterson. Mr McLaren baptised Lilian at Lendrum.

52   The cow and her calf, with John Mair the milkman, who took her back to Lendrum from Millmoss after the 'riot' in Turriff in 1914.

53   Mrs Paterson with the Turra Coo and her calf in 1916.

54   The Coo and her calf with John Mair in 1916.

TURRA COO TRIAL. THE DOG THAT CHASED THE COO.

55   The dog that chased the Coo. Per Mrs E Hutchison, Peterhead.

had it for a long time. The mans name is Johnnie Wilson and he lived in an auld thatched hoose at the roadside at Turfhill New Deer I mind on him fine yet he was a drover between Maud & Turriff and I was Just a little loon. I am also sending you a photo of the Coo as I have it. You can send them back sometime. I thought it might Just interest you or Joggle someone elses memory. I am not a stranger to Turriff as I worked at Yonderton for a number of years during the war. I do hope this interests you . . .[56]

3. The Literature of the Turra Coo

The Turra Coo and all it stood for has so caught the popular mind that a flow of rhymes has continued. The examples given here are the ones so far noted, though there may be more. Although none is of much literary quality, nevertheless they reflect the way in which elements of popular culture may be turned into rhyme or jocular prose. They then become more memorable.

THE TURRA COO

Some tales are false fae en' to en';
But this my tale is true;
You maybe havna heard as yet
Aboot The Turra' Coo.

Her Maister wadna pay the tax,
Although he kent it due;
The higher pooers to Lendrum gaed,
An' there they pinned a coo.

They tried 'im sair to lick the stamps,
But that he wadna do;
They tried 'im syne to pay a fine,
An' syne they took the coo.

They led 'er to the Turra' Square
To meet the public view;
But nae a sowl would gie a bid
To buy the Lendrum coo.

A noisy crood cam' roon;
The din yet lood an' looder grew;
The 'Riot Act' micht weel been read
Aboot the Turra' coo.

The rowdies cut the tow in twa
In spite o' men in blue;
An' syne she ran to save her skin—
You couldna blame the coo.

The auctioneer took to his heels,
An' soon was lost to view;
He saw he needna try that day
To sell the Turra' coo.

They took 'er a' to Aberdeen;
Her journey known to few;
But nae a sowl as yet can tell
Fa bocht the Turra' coo.[57]

THE FAMOUS TURRA COO

Some have upon the battle-plain
Won everlasting fame.
Some have upon the field of sport
Linked laurels to their name:
But beasts, as well as men comprise
The world's 'Remembered Few'.
If me you doubt, here is my proof.
The famous Turra Coo.

Now, Patterson of Lendrum was
A man of sense and tact.
But he refused compliance with
The new Insurance Act.
He had been fined in court, and yet.
He never would subdue:
Hence in the limelight did appear
The famous Turra Coo.

The agents who are paid to see
This Act is carried out,
Conferred, but failed to understand.
What Robert was about.

They were sometimes quite at a loss
To know just what to do.
But finally they did decide
To 'poind' the Turra Coo.

They next did notify the police
Just as to what they meant.
And then for Gordon, auctioneer.
Of Auchtermuchtie sent.
A warrant of distress secures,
(Signed by the Sheriff too),
Then advertised the fact they'd 'roup'
The famous Turra Coo.

The day of days at last arrived.
To Lendrum 'toon' went they.
'Authority on lue' [sic] displayed
To Robert they did say.
'Comply with the Insurance Act,
That's what you'll have to do,
Or else by virtue of the same,
We'll seize the Turra Coo.'

Bold Robert smiled, then firmly said,
'I owe not any man.
And every time, for needy folk,
I do the best I can.
But to conform with such an Act,
That's what I'll never do.
So you can seize, and sell at will
The famous Turra Coo'.

Accordingly they haltered her,
And led her from the byre.
A hostile crowd had gathered there,
And someone shouted 'fire'.
Then in an instant ancient eggs,
Like showers of hailstones flew:
Well 'fertilized' were brand new togs,
But not the Turra Coo.

Brave Sergeant Scott, with squads of police,
Dame Whitie's escort formed.
But they, with clods and putrid spuds,
Were next, and fiercely stormed.
And yet the orders of their Chief
They closely did pursue
But closer did they follow up
The famous Turra Coo.

At last they reached the market place,
The milling mob increased:
'How much now,' asked the auctioneer,
'How much for this fine beast?'
The words had scarcely left his lips,
When mud-pies at him flew,
But Gordon wagged his fists and roared,
'Who'll buy the Turra Coo?'

At length a neighbour made a bid,
But very low it was:
This from the rowdy rounders brought
A hearty loud applause.
'I thank you,' snapped the auctioneer,
'But tight as a clam are you:
A decent price I must have for
The famous Turra Coo.'

'Come on, Come on,' continued John,
'Give me an honest bid:
This animal gives milk like soanes,
She's worth a dozen quid.
When sick or hurt there's no one should
Be living "han-to-moo":
Bid high, the sky's the limit for
The famous Turra Coo.'

But matters got from bad to worse.
The crowd more violent grew:
Stones, lumps of earth, and chunks of woo'
In all directions flew.
With tail on high, and foaming mouth,

The streets she vanished through
Nor did she halt to say 'farewell',
The famous Turra Coo.

The sale was made, who purchased her
None present seemed to know.
But he to whom she was 'knocked down'
Scotch spirit true did show.
For only two days after that
This did he quietly do.
Present the dauntless Robert with
His famous Turra Coo.[58]

THE SELLIN' O' THE 'FITE COO'
On Reading the Account of Tuesday's Scene at Turriff

Losh be here! Fat's this Aw see?
Has Turra clean gein on th' spree?
Or fat the sorra ails them a'?
Sic ongyans fegs, Aw never saw!
Aw doot they've tastit something ilk
Than drappies o' the 'Fite Coo's' milk;
They've maybe tried th' aul' 'Black Bull',
An' o' th' milk ha'e drunk their full.
Bit a' that's nayther here nor there;
For sic details we dinna care.
Bit, sal! Ah'm awfu' wae t' see
Th' silly cantrip, that they dee—
They're lauchin'-stocks t'ilky toon
Besides th' hail wide country roon—
Fan ony Legislature Ack
Jist lays them clean upon their back.
Aw'm sure we a' ha'e trials t' bear
An' ilka ane has his ain bit care;
An' yet, for a', we dinna droon
Oor cares in drink, an' vrack th' toon,
Th' Insurance Ack has passed t' law,
An' Aw' regret wi' ye a',
Bit Aw' hinna taent that vera ill

As t' qualifee for Elmhill.
Rich' weel you fairmer chiels I ken
It's in ye're pooch ye ha'e th' pain.
An' here ye gar th' servants pause
T' see ye fechtin' for their cause.
Peer chiels! if they wid only think
It's nae for them bit for th' 'clink'
That kwytes are thrown upon the green!
Bit some day it will a' be seen
Oh! noo, for Turra's sake, gyang hame,
An', dinna ever try th' same;
They'll say that, like her steens, ye're saft,
Folk says already that she's daft.
But if ye wint t' dance ye're jigs,
There's plenty room on Lendrum's rigs.
For ye can ramp, an' rage, an' roar,
An' bann Lloyd George for evermore.

THE TURRA COO

Feck o fowk in Turra toon
On State Insurance cuist a frown
An' some on it their fit put doon
They widna lick the stamp O.

Roun' Lendrum wey the chiels did swear
'We'll stamp nae cairds, but keep our gear'
Out Turra wards their debt to clear
They started on their tramp O.

Chorus
For there the coo, the Turra Coo.
The Lendrum fowk maun forfeit noo
It's Turra toon the day, I troo
For cattleman and grieve O.

O Here's the coo, the Turra Coo
Unwittin' cause o a the stew
Still yielding to nae function
Like sellin' by unction
The fite coo o' Turra's awa' noo.

A fleggit beast, the square upon
Wi skirls an' lauchter goaded on
Did turn her tail to salesman's Sam
An' loupin', tearin' lang the road
An trampit thru the toon O.

Thro shooers and aul kail runts and sod
Wi stick or knieve an' antrin prod
To Lendrum turned her roun O.

To Aberdeen puir crummie came
Preceded by her Turra fame
To sell her 'twas a woefu shame'.
They'd hae anither try O.

Expectant crood is stanin' near
But gates are shut an void o' steer
Wi just a dizzen loons to hear
Oor public Sale is bye O.
O' far's the coo etc [59]

THE TURRA COO

(Air: 'The Rowan Tree')

O Turra Coo, O Turra Coo
Yer like we never saw,
Entwined's thy name wi mony men
Wha're weel kent in the law.
Yer fame has spread frae pole to pole
Ye are fair Turra's pride
There ne'er wis sic a weel kent coo
In a the countryside
                    O Turra Coo.

On Lendrum's braes in simmer days
Ye pu'ed the grass sae green
Bit since that time on Turra square
Ye roudy sichts hae seen

An thy white hide bore mony names
Sarcastic . . . we'll alloo . . .
And they're engraven on our minds
And on the Shirra's too
                    O Turra Coo.

We stood aroon ye on the Square
The day they tried the Sale
Ye took a notion in yer heid
And fairly turned tail.
An' 'Drachlaw', Oh, I see him yet
A rocket in his han'
He cried 'Boo, Boo' and after you
Wi' a his micht he ran
                    O Turra Coo.

The sequel to this little tale
Wis heard in Aiberdeen
'Not Proven' was the verdict
An' there's 'bonnets' on the green
Lang may ye roam oer your new hame
Midst clovery pastures too
For naething in the Bovine race
Matched the Turra Coo
                    O Turra Coo. [60]

CHILDREN'S JINGLE AT GAMES

Itchie Moo
Ye're affa Blue
Jist like the Turra Coo.[61]

THE TURRA COO

This is the tale o' the Turra coo,
It caused an afa how dye do,
The story gaed the World roon,
And brocht some fame tae Turra toon.

Lloyd George was Prime Minister then,
He wished tae help his fellow men,
Sae he declared that ane an' a',
Should stamp a card—that was the law.

But ae man that law he didna heed,
He didna dae it oot o' greed,
Rob Paterson o' Lendrum fairm,
Just thocht it wad dae less guid . . . mair hairm.

Sae fan his debts began tae grow,
They took awa his guid fat coo.
They trailt her doon tae Turra Square,
Arranged a special auction there.

The croods they cam frae far and near,
The noise was deafenin' tae hear.
The coo took fleg and tossed her heid,
Ran through the square at sic a speed.

But freedom wis ower hard tae fin'.
They catched her fin she lost her win',
And sent her off tae Aiberdeen.
Now this was in the year '13.

There Robbie's freens they bocht her neist.
For seven pound, gaed Rob his beast
Sae back tae Lendrum cam this coo.
The cause o' a' the hullabaloo.[62]

TURRA COO

On Lendrum's braes for mony days
She pood the girss so green.
Oh Turra Coo! Oh Turra Coo!
Your fame is widely spread.

Another version:

On Lendrum's braes in summer days
Ye pee'd [sic] the grass sae green,

But since that time on Turra Square
Ye rowdy sichts hae seen
An thy white hide bore mony names
Sarcastic we'll alloo . . .
And they're engraven on our minds
And on the Shirra's too
O Turra Coo.[63]

THE TURRA COO

1 I saw a story in the Sunday Post
   So I thocht I'd write tae you
   And send you this wee bit o Poem
   Composed tae the Turra Coo.

2 My stepfather he wis Georgie Black
   And fin he wis jist a loon
   It was him that helped tae drive the Coo
   Tae the mart at Turra Toon.

3 I often heard him tell the tale
   Fin I wis jist a quine
   Aboot the selling o the Coo
   Your story brocht [sic] it back tae mind.

4 The Sherriff Officers they came
   And took the Coo awa
   Because Robbie Paterson the fairmer
   Widna pey insurance stamps ata.

5 But when the Coo was in the mart
   There wis sic an affa soon
   The Turriff folk bocht back the Coo
   And Took her Back tae Lendrum Toon.

6 The Turra coo will aye be famous
   And will live in memory
   For noo it will stand upon a statue
   For a the Folks tae see.

7   Because a monument will be erected
    Planned and built by you
    In memory of the Legend
    O the famous Turra Coo.

8   Robbie Paterson would be gey prood
    Tae ken that folk will mind
    Aboot what happened tae the Turra Coo
    In the days o auld Lang Syne.[64]

THE CHRONICLES OF THE TURRA COO

And behold, on the second year, in the reign of King George, there went forth a decree, Let every Master and Mistress pay for a manservant, 3 pieces of copper every seventh day, and for each maid servant 3 pieces of copper likewise: and let every manservant pay 4 pieces of copper every seventh day and every maidservant 3 pieces of copper. For behold there be much sickness in the land, and thus shall each man be prepared against the day of sickness. That a man cunning in the use of herbs be at his bedside and likewise unto each man that is sick shall be paid 10 pieces of silver, and unto every woman likewise 7 and a $\frac{1}{2}$ pieces: and behold unto every woman that travaileth shall 30 pieces be paid.

And behold a cry arose throughout the land, and those of the tribe of Tory were much incensed against the King's Minister which is called David. Now the King's Minister was a radical and some of the men of his tribe were wroth and joined themselves unto the men of Tory. And from Dan to Bersheba there was much weeping and wailing and they said.

'Behold we perish'—'Our burdens are more than we can bear.' Did not the Minister called Austin lash us with whips and did not we reject him and cast him forth and lo! now scourge us with scorpions. But the hearts of the men of those days were like unto water, until there arose in the Far North a man called Robert of the town of Turriff or Turra, for the people of that region spake in uncouth tongue. And Robert was like Gideon of old a tiller of the soil and he sent and called his neighbours from the stables and from the reaping hook and from the threshing floor: and a mighty concourse, numerous as the sands of the sea shore, assembled themselves in the market place and with a noise like the rushing of many waters and with the clapping of hands they swore with great oath that they would not pay the publicans the smallest part of the tax, nae not even to one farthing. And there was a great drought in the land and many men had quenched their thirst with fiery liquers and waxed eloquent in council. But in secret the hearts of many did quail with fear and trembling took hold of them and they communed within themselves.

Doth not this man David eat up our substance? Hath he not taken our belongings and shall he not take much more per-adventure we anger him. Therefore let us pay tribute lest worse befalls us. But Robert was not moved—and the Judge of that land did order that one of his cows be sold in the market place by the tax gatherers; and on that day ordained by a judge a great multitude like unto the stars of the firmament for numbers did gather themselves in the market place; and at the sixth hour, nine of the King's men of great stature and apparel in blue, led the cow: while the snows (sons) of Anat upon the market place. And a magician smote the poind with his staff in his hand and lo there issued forth a tongue of flame with noise of thunder and the men came from all sides to see the wonder and the crush was so great that the cow was loosed from her halter and she did run for fear.

And the heart of our Samuel, vendor of cows did melt from fear and he hid himself in a stable: and the men in the assembly did make offerings to him of clay and succulent plants of the garden and of eggs that stank. But he wot not that these were peace offerings for the men of that region are a barbarous people. And the King's officers waxed wroth and Robert with seven of his followers with blowing of rams' horns and music of pipes and drums, which made noise of pigs before a slaughter. And it was much marvelled that the walls of that city did not fall like unto the walls of Jericho when stormed by Joshua.

—But David still remained Minister to the King—

TO THE TURRA COO

Ye may labour yer wife to the edge o' her life,
Steal the sleepers and rails off the line,
Even 'Five' may be wrote on a One Pound Note,
Ye'll get aff wi' a nominal fine,
But lend doon yer ear, and attentively hear,
What liberal authority says.
'Ye daurna say Boo tae the Lendrum Coo,
For fear ye get sixty days.'[65]

4   Robert Paterson's Family

Robert's parents were James Paterson and Elspeth Brodie.
He and his wife Margaret Reid had five children:

Elspeth Brodie (died 1986).

Alfrida Frances, Turriff.

Margaret Elizabeth, Sussex, who married the late Dr Frederick Hunter, formerly of Towie House, Turriff.

Lilian Mary, who married Dr Alexander Hunter (brother of Frederick), now in Canada.

George Paterson (died 1966).

References

1 Details about the history of Turriff are neatly summarised in J D Dempster, *Turriff o'er the Centuries, 500AD–1913AD* (Turriff and District Heritage Society, 1982).

2 Quoted in S Wood, *The Shaping of 19th Century Aberdeenshire* (Stevenage, 1985) p 68.

3 *Old (First) Statistical Account of Scotland*, Vol 17 (1794–5) p 401.

4 J Gordon, *History of Scots Affairs from 1637 to 1641* (Spalding Club, Aberdeen 1841) II, p 259. J Spalding, *Memorialls of the Trubles in Scotland and in England 1624–1645* (Spalding Club, Aberdeen 1850) I, pp 136 ff; See also A Smith, *A New History of Aberdeenshire* (Aberdeen II, 1875) pp 1331–4.

5 I J Simpson, *Education in Aberdeenshire before 1872* (London, 1947).

6 J D Dempster (1982) p 17.

7 R Southey, *Tour in Scotland in 1819* (Edinburgh, 1972).

8 For the broad background, see, e.g. E J Hobsbawm, *Industry and Empire* (London, 1984) p 239; W Ferguson, *Scotland 1689 to the Present* (Edinburgh and London, 1968), pp 345 ff; I G C Hutchison, *A Political History of Scotland 1832–1924. Elections and Issues* (Edinburgh, 1986), p 256; J F C Harrison, *The Common People. A History from the Norman Conquest to the Present* (Fontana Press, 1984, 1989 ed) pp 344–5.

9 D Stevenson, ed, *Reminiscences of an Unlettered Man, Robert Barclay, 1850–1927* (Aberdeen, 1985), p 71.

10 e.g. John McCallum, *The Great Betrayal. The Fraud of Compulsory Insurance, and How to Get Rid of It*, with an introduction by Hilaire Belloc. It cost 1*d*.

11 See *Record of Events in Aberdeen and the North 1801–1927 (Aberdeen Press and Journal)*, Aberdeen 1928.

12 *Aberdeen Journal*, 11 December 1913.

13 Reports—1914. 2 Scots Law Times, pp 11–15; *North British Agriculturist*, 21 January 1915, p 35; 28 January, p 59; 18 March, p 179; 5 August, p 508.

14 *The Scottish Farming News*, 25 October 1913, p 12.

15 *Turriff and District Advertiser*, 3 September 1971.

16 I A N Henderson, 'The Turra Coo', in *The Scots Magazine*, December 1971, pp 223–4; *North British Agriculturist*, 15 January 1914, p 45.

17 *The Scottish Farm Servant*, January 1914, p 24.

18 *Ibid.*, February 1914, p 6.

19 Scottish Record Office, CS252/800; *North British Agriculturist*, 11 December 1913, p 837.

20   A McKay, 'Turra Coo' Riot Case was 50 Years Ago. In *Aberdeen Press and Journal*, July 1963.
21   *Turriff and District Advertiser*, 25 August 1978.
22   *The Scottish Farm Servant*, January 1914, p 24.
23   *Ibid.*, April 1914, p 11.
24   *Ibid.*, March 1914, p 2.
25   *Ibid.*, April 1914, p 14.
26   *North British Agriculturist*, 15 January 1914, p 45.
27   *Ibid.*, 15 January 1914, p 45.
28   *Ibid.*, 11 December 1913, p 837; 15 January 1914, p 45.
29   *Ibid.*, 15 December 1913, p 837; 15 January 1914, p 45.
30   Scottish Record Office, Court of Session CS 252/800, and CS252/800/2.
31   *North British Agriculturist*, 25 December 1913, p 873.
32   *The Evening Gazette*, 9 January 1914; *North British Agriculturist*, 8 January 1914, p 19.
33   *North British Agriculturist*, 15 January 1914, p 45.
34   Letter in the possession of Alex Winton, Turriff.
35   *The Aberdeen Daily Journal*, 21 January 1914, p 5; see also I A N Henderson, 'The Turra Coo', in *The Scots Magazine*, December 1971, p 229.
36   *The Scottish Farming News*, 25 October 1913, p 7.
37   *North British Agriculturist*, 3 June 1915, p 358.
38   Scottish Record Office, Court of Session CS252/800/4.
39   *North British Agriculturist*, 12 February, 1914, p 111.
40   *Ibid.*, 10 December 1914, p 805.
41   *Ibid.*, 15 July 1915, p 453.
42   Letter, Catherine H Adam to Miss E B Paterson, 2 May 1971, kindly made available by Agnes Ritchie.
43   Letter, John A Harvie-Brown to a friend, 5 February 1914; copy drawn to my attention by Miss E B Paterson.
44   The remainder of this letter, dealing with the bad effects of using turpentine to clean slogans off the cow, is given earlier (pp 14–15).
45   Letter made available by Alex Winton.
46   George Paterson, who took a keen interest in the activities of his younger brother, and who had for a time encouraged him to emigrate, was an enterprising merchant in Liverpool. He helped to found the Liverpool Scottish and was a city councillor in Liverpool.
47   It was Mrs Mitchell who painted the portrait in oils presented to him by the North of Scotland Home Timber Merchants' Association, of which he was President for 6 years.
48   Much of the above information on Robert Paterson is based on notes kindly supplied by his daughter, the late Miss E B Paterson.
49   *Turriff and District Advertiser*, 5 November 1971.
50   *The Scottish Farm Servant*, February 1914, p 2.

51 J H Smith, *Joe Duncan. The Scottish Farm Servants and British Agriculture* (RCSS, University of Edinburgh, and the Scottish Labour History Society), Edinburgh, 1973, p 32, 34–5.

52 I Carter, *Farm Life in Northeast Scotland 1840–1914*, (Edinburgh 1979) pp 172–3.

53 C W Hill, *Edwardian Scotland* (New Jersey, 1976) p 120. The same volume (p 128) refers to the use of a white cow, almost in anticipation of the Turra Coo, on a Liberal election poster. It shows a train marked '1909 Budget' speeding towards a white cow in the middle of the track. The cow wears a ducal coronet, since at this date the Liberals were intent on abusing the House of Lords, and especially the Dukes in it. The words on the poster were 'George Stephenson was once asked if it would not be awkward if a cow were to place itself on the line in front of a train. "Yes," promptly replied the great man, "it would indeed be awkward—for the cow".'

54 A Fenton, 'Goverment Action and Popular Reaction. A Twentieth Century Episode in the Northeast of Scotland', in N A Bringéus *et al.*, eds, *Wandel der Volkskultur in Europa* (Münster, 1988), I, pp 89–103; A Fenton, 'Popular culture and the Turra Coo', in G Cruickshank, ed, *A Sense of Place. Studies in Scottish Local History* (Edinburgh, 1988), pp 76–86. The latter article was reviewd by Neal Ascherson in *Observer Scotland*, 19 March 1989.

55 Henderson, *op. cit.*, pp 227–9.

56 Letter made available by Alex Winton.

57 Provided by Mrs Alexander Grant, Craigielea, and reprinted in *The Story of 'The Turra Coo'* (W Peters & Son Ltd, 16 High Street, Turriff), undated.

58 Composed by Sergeant W D Milne, Police Department New Westminster BC, Canada.

59 By 'An Aul' Turra Loon, Aberdeen 10.12.1913'. This is probably the earliest versified response to the episode. The quality of the dialect is strikingly good.

60 According to a note by Miss Paterson, this is dated 12 January 1914. It is by T L Morrison, Town Chamberlain, Inverurie.

61 In Lewis Grassic Gibbon's *Sunset Song*, first published in 1932, reference is made in the Prelude to Erbert Ellison, the Irish manager of the Kinraddie estate Mains farm, a known Tory. The bairns would shout at him:
'Inky poo, your nose is blue,
You're awful like the Turra Coo,
'. . . for he'd sent a subscription to the creature up Turriff way whose cow had been sold to pay his Insurance, and folk said it was no more than a show off, the Cow creature and Ellison both' Pan Books edn, 1973, p 7). Gibbon's real name was James Leslie Mitchell; he was born in Auchterless in 1901.

62 Written by the children of Ardmiddle School, and reproduced in the *Aberdeen Press and Journal*, 29 July 1978.

63 Second version in the *Aberdeen Press and Journal*, 29 July 1978.

64 Written by Mrs Madge Gall, New Pitsligo, and sent to Alexander Winton at

Lendrum, following her reading of the *Sunday Post* article on 11 April 1971. Her letter reads: 'Dear Mr Winton, Seeing the story in the Sunday Post about the Turra Coo I take this opportunity of sending you a Poem Composed by me I write Poetry in my spare time as a hobby so thought you might like one about the Turra Coo'.

65   This piece of prose and verse came to Alex Winton from Alex Taylor in Perth (born in Auchterless), about 1968.